Adobe After Effects Keyboard Shortcuts for Windows and Macintosh OS

By

U. C-Abel Books.

Table of Contents

Acknowledgement.

All thanks to God Almighty for enabling us to bring this work to this point. He is a wonder indeed.

We want to specially appreciate the great company, Adobe Systems for their hard work and style of reasoning when it comes to providing the public with helpful programs and resources, and for helping us with some of the tips and keyboard shortcuts included in this book.

Dedication

The dedication of this title goes to users of Adobe After Effects all over the world.

How We Began.

We enjoy using shortcuts because they set us on a high plane that astonishes people around us when we work with them. As wonderful shortcuts users, the worst eyesore we witness in computer operation is to see somebody sluggishly struggling to execute a task through mouse usage when in actual sense shortcuts will help to save that person time. Most people have asked us to help them with a list of keyboard shortcuts that can make them work as smartly as we do and that drove us into research to broaden our knowledge and truly help them as they demanded, that is the reason for the existence of this book. It is a great tool for lovers of shortcuts, and those who want to join the group.

Most times the things we love don't come by easily. It is our love for keyboard shortcuts that made us to bear long sleepless nights like owls just to make sure we get the best out of it, and it is the best we got that we are sharing with you in this book. You cannot be the same at computing after reading this book. The time you entrusted to our care is an expensive possession and we promise not to mess it up.

Thank you.

What to Know Before You Begin.

General Notes.

1. Most of the keyboard shortcuts you will see in this book refer to the U.S. keyboard layout. Keys for other layouts might not correspond exactly to the keys on a U.S. keyboard. Keyboard shortcuts for laptop computers might also differ.

2. It is important to note that when using shortcuts to perform any command, you should make sure the target area is active, if not, you may get a wrong result. Example, if you want to highlight all texts you must make sure the text field is active and if an object, make sure the object area is active. The active area is always known by the location where the cursor of your computer blinks.

3. On a Mac keyboard, the Command key is denoted with the ⌘ symbol.

4. If a function key doesn't work on your Mac as you expect it to, press the Fn key in addition to the function key. If you don't want to press the Fn key every time, you can change your Apple system preferences.

5. The plus (+) sign that comes in the middle of keyboard shortcuts simply means the keys are

meant to be combined or held down together not to be added as one of the shortcut keys. In a case where plus sign is needed; it will be duplicated (++).

6. Many keyboards assign special functions to function keys, by default. To use the function key for other purposes, you have to press Fn+the function key.

7. For keyboard shortcuts in which you press one key immediately followed by another key, the keys are separated by a comma (,).

8. For chapters that have more than one topic, search for "A fresh topic" to see the beginning of a topic, and "End of Topic" to see the end of a topic.

9. It is also important to note that the keyboard shortcuts, tips, and techniques listed in this book are for users of Adobe After Effects.

10. To get more information on this title visit ucabelbooks.wordpress.com and search the site using keywords related to it.

11. Our chief website is under construction.

Some Short Forms You Will Find in This Book and Their Full Meaning.

Here are short forms used in this Adobe After Effects Keyboard Shortcuts for Windows and Macintosh OS book and their full meaning.

1. Win   -   Windows logo key
2. Tab   -   Tabulate Key
3. Shft   -   Shift Key
4. Prt sc   -   Print Screen
5. Num Lock   -   Number Lock Key
6. F   -   Function Key
7. Esc   -   Escape Key
8. Ctrl   -   Control Key
9. Caps Lock   -   Caps Lock Key
10. Alt   -   Alternate Key

CHAPTER 1.

Fundamental Knowledge of Keyboard Shortcuts.

Without the existence of the keyboard, there wouldn't have been anything like keyboard shortcuts so in this chapter we will learn a little about the computer keyboard before moving to keyboard shortcuts.

1. Definition of Computer Keyboard.

This is an input device that is used to send data to computer memory.

Sketch of a Keyboard

1.1 Types of Keyboard.

   i. Standard (Basic) Keyboard.

  ii. Enhanced (Extended) Keyboard.

   i. **Standard Keyboard:** This is a keyboard designed during the 1800s for mechanical typewriters with just 10 function keys (F keys) placed at the left side of it.

  ii. **Enhanced Keyboard:** This is the current 101 to 102-key keyboard that is included in almost all the personal computers (PCs) of nowadays, which has 12 function keys, usually at the top side of it.

Function Keys

Numeric Keys

Alphabetic keys

1.2 Segments of the keyboard

- Numeric keys.
- Alphabetic keys.
- Punctuation keys.
- Windows Logo key.
- Function keys.
- Special keys.

Numeric Keys: Numeric keys are keys with numbers from **0 - 9**.

Alphabetic Keys: These are keys that have alphabets on them, ranging from **A** to **Z**.

Punctuation Keys: These are keys of the keyboard used for punctuation, examples include comma, full stop, colon, question marks, hyphen, etc.

Windows Logo Key: A key on Microsoft Computer keyboard with its logo displayed on it. Search for this ⊞ on your keyboard.

Apple Key: This also known as Command key is a modifier key that you can find on an Apple keyboard. It usually has the image of an apple or command logo on it. Search for this on your Apple keyboard

Function Keys: These are keys that have **F** on them which are usually combined with other keys. They are F1 - F12, and are also in the class called *Special Keys*.

Special Keys: These are keys that perform special functions. They include: Tab, Ctrl, Caps lock, Insert, Prt sc, alt gr, Shift, Home, Num lock, Esc, and many others. Special keys differ according to the type of computer involved. In some keyboard layout, especially laptops, the keys that turn the speaker on/off, the one that increases/decreases volume, the key that turns the computer Wifi on/off are also special keys.

Other Special Keys Worthy of Note.

Enter Key: This is located at the right-hand corner of most keyboards. It is used to send messages to the computer to execute commands, in most cases it is used to mean "Ok" or "Go".

Escape Key (ESC): This is the first key on the upper left of most keyboards. It is used to cancel routines, close menus and select options such as **Save** according to circumstances.

Control Key (CTRL): It is located on the bottom row of the left and right hand side of the keyboard. They also work with the function keys to execute commands using Keyboard shortcuts (key combinations).

Alternate Key (ALT): It is located on the bottom row also of some keyboard, very close to the CTRL key on both side of the keyboard. It enables many editing functions to be accomplished by using some keystroke combinations on the keyboard.

Shift Key: This adds to the roles of function keys. In addition, it enables the use of alternative function of a particular button (key), especially, those with more than one function on a key. E.g. use of capital letters, symbols, and numbers.

1.3. Selecting/Highlighting With Keyboard.

This is a highlighting method or style where data is selected using the computer keyboard instead of a computer mouse.

To do this:

- Move your cursor to the text or object you want to highlight, make sure that area is active,
- Hold down the shift key with one finger,
- Then use another finger to move the arrow key that points to the direction you want to highlight.

1.4 The Operating Modes Of The Keyboard.

Just like the computer mouse, keyboard has two operating modes. The two modes are Text Entering Mode and Command Mode.

a. **Text Entering Mode:** this mode gives the operator/user the opportunity to type text.
b. **Command Mode:** this is used to command the operating system/software/application to execute commands in certain ways.

2. Ways To Improve In Your Typing Skill.

1. Put Your Eyes Off The Keyboard.

This is the aspect of keyboard usage that many don't find funny because they always ask. "How can I put my eyes off the keyboard when I am running away from the occurrence of errors on my file?" My aim is to be fast, is this not going to slow me down?

Of course, there will be errors and at the same time your speed will slow down but the motive behind the introduction to this method is to make you faster than you are. Looking at your keyboard while you type can make you get a sore neck, it is better you learn to touch type because the more you type with your eyes fixed on the screen instead of the keyboard, the faster you become.

An alternative to keeping your eyes off your keyboard is to use the *"Das Keyboard Ultimate"*.

2. Errors Challenge You

It is better to fail than to not try at all. Not trying at all is an attribute of the weak and lazybones. When you make mistakes, try again because errors are opportunities for improvement.

3. Good Posture (Position Yourself Well).

Do not adopt an awkward position while typing. You should get everything on your desk organized or arranged before sitting to type. Your posture while typing contributes to your speed and productivity.

4. Practice

Here is the conclusion of everything said above. You have to practice your shortcuts constantly. The practice alone is a way of improvement. "Practice brings improvement". Practice always.

2.1 Software That Will Help You Improve Your Typing Skill.

There are several Software programs for typing that both kids and adults can use for their typing skill. Here is a list of software that can help you improve in your typing: Mavis Beacon, Typing Instructor, Mucky Typing Adventure, Rapid Tying Tutor, Letter Chase Tying Tutor, Alice Touch Typing Tutor and many more. Personally, I love Mavis Beacon.

To learn typing using MAVIS BEACON, install Mavis Beacon software to your computer, start with keyboard lesson, then move to games. Games like **Penguin Crossing, Creature Lab**, or **Space Junk** will help you become a professional in typing. Typing and keyboard shortcuts work hand-in-hand.

Sketch of a computer mouse

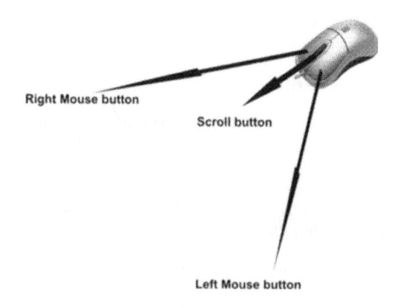

Right Mouse button

Scroll button

Left Mouse button

3. Mouse:

This is an oval-shaped portable input device with three buttons for scrolling, left clicking, and right clicking that enables work to be done effectively on a computer. The plural form of mouse is mice.

3.1 Types of Computer Mouse

- Mechanical Mouse.
- Optical Mechanical Mouse (Optomechanical).
- Laser Mouse.

- Optical Mouse.
- BlueTrack Mouse.

3.2 Forms of Clicking:

Left Clicking: This is the process of clicking the left side button of the mouse. It can also be called *clicking* without the addition of *left*.

Right Clicking: It is the process of clicking the right side button of a computer mouse.

Double Clicking: It is the process of clicking the left side button two times (twice) and immediately.

Triple Clicking: It is the process of clicking the left side button three times (thrice) and immediately.

Double clicking is used to select a word while triple clicking is used to select a sentence or paragraph.

Scroll Button: It is the little key attached to the mouse that looks like a tiny wheel. It takes you up and down a page when moved.

3.3 Mouse Pad: This is a small soft mat that is placed under the mouse to make it have a free movement.

3.4 Laptop Mouse Touchpad

This unlike the mouse we explained above is not external, rather it is inbuilt (comes with the laptop computer). With the presence of a laptop mouse touchpad, an external mouse is not needed to use a laptop, except in a case where it is malfunctioning or the operator prefers to use external one for some reasons.

The laptop mouse touchpad is usually positioned at the end of the keyboard section of a laptop computer. It is rectangular in shape with two buttons positioned below it. The two buttons/keys are used for left and right clicking just like the external mouse. Some laptops come with four mouse keys. Two placed above the mouse for left and right clicking and two other keys placed below it for the same function.

4. Definition Of Keyboard Shortcuts.

Keyboard shortcuts are defined as a series of keys, most times with combination that execute tasks which typically involve the use of mouse or other input devices.

5. Why You Should Use Shortcuts.

1. One may not be able to use a computer mouse easily because of disability or pain.

2. One may not be able to see the mouse pointer as a result of vision impairment, in such case what will the person do? The answer is SHORTCUT.

3. Research has made it known that Extensive mouse usage is related to Repetitive Syndrome Injury (RSI) greatly than the use of keyboard.

4. Keyboard shortcuts speed up computer users, making learning them a worthwhile effort.

5. When performing a job that requires precision, it is wise that you use the keyboard instead of mouse, for instance, if you are dealing with Text Editing, it is better you handle it using keyboard shortcuts than spending more time doing it with your computer mouse alone.

6. Studies calculate that using keyboard shortcuts allows working 10 times faster than working with the mouse. The time you spend looking for the mouse and then getting the cursor to the position you want is lost! Reducing your work duration by 10 times gives you greater results.

5.1 Ways To Become A Lover Of Shortcuts.

1. Always have the urge to learn new shortcut keys associated with the programs you use.
2. Be happy whenever you learn a new shortcut.

3. Try as much as you can to apply the new shortcuts you learnt.
4. Always bear it in mind that learning new shortcuts is worth it.
5. Always remember that the use of keyboard shortcuts keeps people healthy while performing computer activities.

5.2 How To Learn New Shortcut Keys

1. Do a research on them: quick references (a cheat sheet comprehensively compiled like ours) can go a long way to help you improve.
2. Buy applications that show you keyboard shortcuts every time you execute an action with mouse.
3. Disconnect your mouse if you must learn this fast.
4. Read user manuals and help topics (Whether offline or online).

5.3 Your Reward For Knowing Shortcut Keys.

1. You will get faster unimaginably.
2. Your level of efficiency will increase.
3. You will find it easy to use.
4. Opportunities are high that you will become an expert in what you do.
5. You won't have to go for **Office button**, click **New,** click **Blank and Recent**, and click **Create**

just to insert a fresh/blank page. **Ctrl +N** takes care of that in a second.

A Funny Note: Keyboarding and Mousing are in a marital union with Keyboarding being the head, so it will be unfair for anybody to put asunder between them.

5.4 Why We Emphasize On The Use of Shortcuts.

You may never leave your mouse completely unless you are ready to make your brain a box of keyboard shortcuts which will really be frustrating, just imagine yourself learning all shortcuts that go with the programs you use and their various versions. You shouldn't learn keyboard shortcuts that way.

Why we are emphasizing on the use of shortcuts is because mouse usage is becoming unusually common and unhealthy, too. So we just want to make sure both are combined so you can get fast, productive and healthy in your computer activities. All you need to know is just the most important ones associated with the programs you use.

CHAPTER 2.

15 (Fifteen) Special Keyboard Shortcuts.

The fifteen special keyboard shortcuts are fifteen (15) shortcuts every computer user should know.

The following is a list of keyboard shortcuts every computer user should know:

1. **Ctrl + A:** Control A, highlights or selects everything you have in the environment where you are working.

    *If you are like **"Wow, the content of this document is large and there is no time to select all of it, besides, it's going to mount pressure on my computer?"** Using the mouse for this is an outdated method of handling a task like selecting all, Ctrl+A will take care of that in a second.*

2. **Ctrl + C:** Control C copies any highlighted or selected element within the work environment.

> *Saves the time and stress which would have been used to right click and click again just to copy. Use ctrl+c.*

3. **Ctrl + N:** Control N opens a new window or file.

> *Instead of clicking* **File, New, blank/ template** *and another* **click,** *just press* ***Ctrl + N*** *and a fresh page or window will* appear instantly.

4. **Ctrl + O:** Control O opens a new program.

> *Use ctrl +O when you want to locate / open a file or program.*

5. **Ctrl + P:** Control P prints the active document.

> *Always use this to locate the printer dialog box, and thereafter print.*

6. **Ctrl + S:** Control S saves a new document or file and changes made by the user.

> *Please stop! Don't use the mouse. Just press Ctrl+S and everything will be saved.*

7. **Ctrl +V:** Control V pastes copied elements into the active area of the program in use.

Using ctrl+V in a case like this Saves the time and stress of right clicking and clicking again just to paste.

8. **Ctrl + W:** Control W is used to close the page you are working on when you want to leave the work environment.

> ***"There is a way Debby does this without using the mouse. Oh my God, why didn't I learn it then?"*** Don't worry, I have the answer. Debby presses Ctrl+W to close active windows.

9. **Ctrl + X:** Control X cuts elements (making the elements to disappear from their original place). The difference between cutting and deleting elements is that in Cutting, what was cut doesn't get lost permanently but prepares itself so that it can be pasted on another location defined by the user.

> *Use ctrl+x when you think **"this shouldn't be here and I can't stand the stress of retyping or redesigning it on the rightful place it belongs".***

10. **Ctrl + Y:** Control Y undoes already done actions.

> *Ctrl+Z brought back what you didn't need? Press Ctrl+ Y to remove it again.*

11. **Ctrl + Z:** Control Z redoes actions.

   Can't find what you typed now or a picture you inserted, it suddenly disappeared or you mistakenly removed it? Press Ctrl+Z to bring it back.

12. **Alt + F4:** Alternative F4 closes active windows or items.

   *You don't need to move the mouse in order to close an active window, just press **Alt + F4**. Also use it when you are done or you don't want somebody who is coming to see what you are doing.*

13. **Ctrl + F6:** Control F6 Navigates between open windows, making it possible for a user to see what is happening in windows that are active.

   Are you working in Microsoft Word and want to find out if the other active window where your browser is loading a page is still progressing? Use Ctrl + F6.

14. **F1:** This displays the help window.

   *Is your computer malfunctioning? Use **F1** to find help when you don't know what next to do.*

15. **F12:** This enables user to make changes to an already saved document.

    F12 is the shortcut to use when you want to change the format in which you saved your existing document, password it, change its name, change the file location or destination, or make other changes to it. It will save you time.

Note: The Control (Ctrl) key on Windows and Linux operating system is the same thing as Command (Cmmd) key on a Macintosh computer. So if you replace Control with Command key on a Mac computer for the special shortcuts listed above, you will get the same result.

CHAPTER 3.

Tips, Tricks, and Keyboard Shortcuts for Use in After Effects.

About the program: This is an industry-standard tool for video composition, motion graphics design, and animation developed by adobe Systems.

A fresh topic ⌐⌐→

How to Improve Performance in After Effects.

You can improve performance by optimizing your computer system, After Effects, your project, and your workflow. Some of the suggestions here improve performance not by increasing rendering speed but by decreasing time that other operations require, such as opening a project.

By far, the best way to improve performance overall is to plan ahead, run early tests of your workflow and output pipeline, and confirm that what you are delivering is what your client actually wants and expects. (Check <u>Planning your work</u>.)

Improve performance before starting After Effects.

- Make sure that you've installed the current version of After Effects, including any available updates. To check for and install updates, choose Help > Updates.
- Make sure that you've installed the latest versions of drivers and plug-ins, especially video card drivers. To download updates for drivers and plug-ins, go to the provider's website.
- Make sure that your system has enough RAM. Optimum performance is achieved with computer systems with at least 2 GB of installed RAM per processor core. See the documentation for your operating system and computer for details on how to check the amount of installed RAM and how to install RAM.
- Quit applications that are not necessary for your work. If you run applications other than those with which After Effects shares a memory pool, and you don't allocate adequate memory to other applications, performance can be greatly reduced when the operating system swaps RAM to the hard disk.
- Stop or pause resource-intensive operations in other applications, such as video previews in Adobe Bridge.

- Make sure that your system includes a display card that supports OpenGL 2.0 or later. Though After Effects can function without it, OpenGL accelerates various types of rendering, including rendering to the screen for previews.
- When possible, keep the source footage files for your project on a fast local disk drive. If your source footage files are on a slow disk drive (or across a slow network connection), then performance will be poor. Ideally, use separate fast local disk drives for source footage files and rendered output.
- A separate fast disk (or disk array) to assign the disk cache folder to, is ideal. Because of their speed, SSDs work well for this function.

Improve performance by optimizing memory, cache, and multiprocessing settings.

- Allocate adequate memory for other applications.
- Enable caching frames to disk for previews by selecting the Enable Disk Cache preference. In After Effects, assign as much space as possible to the Disk Cache folder (on a separate fast drive) for best performance. See Disk cache.

Improve performance using Global Performance Cache | CC, CS6.

Import projects from After Effects CS5.5 and earlier into After Effects to take advantage of the Global Performance Cache.

Persistent disk cache improves performance by retaining frames stored in the disk cache between sessions, saving rendering time as you work on a project or other projects that might use the same cached frames.

Improve performance by simplifying your project.

By simplifying and dividing your project, you can prevent After Effects from using memory and other resources to process elements that you are not currently working with. Also, by controlling when After Effects performs certain processing, you can greatly improve overall performance. For example, you can avoid repeating an action that needs to happen only once, or you can postpone an action until it is more convenient for you.

- Delete unused elements from your project.
- Divide complex projects into simpler projects, and then recombine them before you render the finished movie. To recombine projects, import all of the projects into a single project.
- Before rendering, put all of your source footage files on a fast, local disk—not the one that you're rendering and exporting to. A good way to do this

is with the Collect Files command. See <u>Collect files in one location</u>.

- Pre-render nested compositions. Render a completed composition as a movie so that After Effects doesn't rerender the composition every time it is displayed.
- Substitute a low-resolution or still-image proxy for a source item when not working directly with that item.
- Lower the resolution for the composition.
- Isolate the layer you're working on by using the Solo switch.

Improve performance by modifying screen output.

You can improve performance in many ways that don't affect how After Effects treats your project data, only how output is drawn to the screen as you work. Although it is often useful to see certain items and information as you work, After Effects uses memory and processor resources to update this information, so be selective in what you choose to display as you work. You will likely need to see different aspects of your project at different points in your workflow, so you may apply the following suggestions in various combinations at various stages.

- Turn off display color management and output simulation when not needed. See <u>Simulate how colors will appear on a different output device</u>.

The speed and quality of color management for previews are controlled by the Viewer Quality preferences.

- Enable hardware acceleration of previews, which uses the GPU to assist in drawing previews to the screen. Choose Edit > Preferences > Display (Windows) or After Effects > Preferences > Display (Mac OS), and select Hardware Accelerate Composition, Layer, And Footage Panels.
- Close unneeded panels. After Effects must use memory and processor resources to update open panels, which may slow the work that you are doing in another panel.
- Create a region of interest. If you are working on a small part of your composition, limit which portion of the composition is rendered to the screen during previews.
- Deselect Show Cache Indicators in the Timeline panel menu to prevent After Effects from displaying green and blue bars in the time ruler to indicate cached frames. See Caches: RAM cache, disk cache, and media cache.
- Deselect the Show Rendering Progress In Info Panel And Flowchart preference to prevent the details of each render operation for each frame from being written to the screen.
- Hide Current Render Details in the Render Queue panel by clicking the triangle beside Current Render Details in the Render Queue panel.

- Press Caps Lock to prevent After Effects from updating Footage, Layer, or Composition panels. When you make a change that would otherwise appear in a panel, After Effects adds a red bar with a text reminder at the bottom of the panel. After Effects continues to update panel controls such as motion paths, anchor points, and mask outlines as you move them. To resume panel updates and display all changes, press Caps Lock again.

Note:

Pressing Caps Lock suspends updates (disables refresh) of previews in viewers during rendering for final output, too, although no red reminder bar appears.

- Lower the display quality of a layer to Draft.
- Select Draft 3D in the Timeline panel menu, which disables all lights and shadows that fall on 3D layers. It also disables the depth-of-field blur for a camera.
- Use fast draft mode while laying out and previewing a ray-traced 3D composition by selecting an option other than "Off" from the Fast Previews button.
- Deselect Live Update in the Timeline panel menu to prevent After Effects from updating compositions dynamically.
- Display audio waveforms in the Timeline panel only when necessary.

- Disable pixel aspect ratio correction by clicking the Toggle Pixel Aspect Ratio Correction button at the bottom of a Composition, Layer, or Footage panel. The speed and quality of pixel aspect ratio correction and other scaling for previews are controlled by the Viewer Quality preferences.
- Deselect Mirror On Computer Monitor when previewing video on an external video monitor.
- Hide layer controls, such as masks, 3D reference axes, and layer handles. See <u>Show or hide layer controls in the Composition panel</u>.
- Lower the magnification for a composition. When After Effects displays the Composition, Layer, and Footage panels at magnifications greater than 100%, screen redraw speed decreases.
- Set the Resolution/Down Sample Factor value of the composition to Auto in the Composition panel, which prevents the unnecessary rendering of rows or columns of pixels that aren't drawn to the screen at low zoom levels.

Improve performance when using effects

Some effects, such as blurs and distortions, require large amounts of memory and processor resources. By being selective about when and how you apply these effects, you can greatly improve overall performance.

- Apply memory-intensive and processor-intensive effects later. Animate your layers and do other work that requires real-time previews before you apply memory-intensive or processor-intensive effects (such as glows and blurs), which may make previews slower than real time.
- Temporarily turn off effects to increase the speed of previews.
- Limit the number of particles generated by particle effects.
- Rather than apply the same effect with the same settings to multiple layers, apply the effect to an adjustment layer. When an effect is applied to an adjustment layer, it is processed once, on the composite of all of the layers beneath it.

End of Topic.

A fresh topic

Keyboard Shortcuts in Adobe After Effects.

Use the following list of keyboard shortcuts to enhance your productivity in Adobe After Effect.

General.

Result	Windows Shortcut	Mac OS Shortcut
Select all	Ctrl+A	Command+A
Deselect all	F2 or Ctrl+Shift+A	F2 or Command+Shift+A
Rename selected layer, compositi on, folder, effect, group, or mask	Enter on main keyboard	Return
Open selected layer, compositi on, or footage item	Enter on numeric keypad	Enter on numeric keypad
Move selected layers, masks, effects, or render items down (back) or	Ctrl+Alt+Dow n Arrow or Ctrl+Alt+Up Arrow	Command+Option+D own Arrow or Command+Option+U p Arrow

up (forward) in stacking order		
Move selected layers, masks, effects, or render items to bottom (back) or top (front) of stacking order	Ctrl+Alt+Shift +Down Arrow or Ctrl+Alt+Shift +Up Arrow	Command+Option+Sh ift+Down Arrow or Command+Option+Sh ift+Up Arrow
Extend selection to next item in Project panel, Render Queue panel, or Effect Controls panel	Shift+Down Arrow	Shift+Down Arrow

Extend selection to previous item in Project panel, Render Queue panel, or Effect Controls panel	Shift+Up Arrow	Shift+Up Arrow
Duplicate selected layers, masks, effects, text selectors, animators, puppet meshes, shapes, render items, output modules, or compositions	Ctrl+D	Command+D

Quit	Ctrl+Q	Command+Q
Undo	Ctrl+Z	Command+Z
Redo	Ctrl+Shift+Z	Command+Shift+Z
Purge All Memory	Ctrl+Alt+/ (on numeric keypad)	Command+Option+/ (on numeric keypad)
Interrupt running a script	Esc	Esc
Display filename corresponding to the frame at the current time in the Info panel	Ctrl+Alt+E	Command+Option+E

Projects.

Result	Windows Shortcut	Mac OS Shortcut
New project	Ctrl+Alt+N	Command+Option+N
Open project	Ctrl+O	Command+O
Open most	Ctrl+Alt+Shift+P	Command+Option+Shift+P

recent project		
New folder in Project panel	Ctrl+Alt+Shift+N	Command+Option+Shift+N
Open Project Settings dialog box	Ctrl+Alt+Shift+K	Command+Option+Shift+K
Find in Project panel	Ctrl+F	Command+F
Cycle through color bit depths for project	Alt-click bit-depth button at bottom of Project panel	Option-click bit-depth button at bottom of Project panel
Open Project Settings dialog box	Click bit-depth button at bottom of Project panel	Click bit-depth button at bottom of Project panel

Preferences.

Result	Windows Shortcut	Mac OS Shortcut
Open Preferences dialog box	Ctrl+Alt+; (semicolon)	Command+Option+; (semicolon)
Restore default preferences settings	Hold down Ctrl+Alt+Shift while starting After Effects	Hold down Command+Option+Shift while starting After Effects

Panels, Viewers, Workspaces, and Windows.

Note:

(Mac OS) Shortcuts involving function keys F9-F12 may conflict with shortcuts used by the operating system. See Mac OS Help for instructions to reassign Dashboard & Expose shortcuts.

Result	Windows Shortcut	Mac OS Shortcut
Open or close Project panel	Ctrl+0	Command+0

Open or close Render Queue panel	Ctrl+Alt+0	Command+Option+0
Open or close Tools panel	Ctrl+1	Command+1
Open or close Info panel	Ctrl+2	Command+2
Open or close Preview panel	Ctrl+3	Command+3
Open or close Audio panel	Ctrl+4	Command+4
Open or close Effects & Presets panel	Ctrl+5	Command+5
Open or close Character panel	Ctrl+6	Command+6
Open or close Paragraph panel	Ctrl+7	Command+7
Open or close Paint panel	Ctrl+8	Command+8

Open or close Brushes panel	Ctrl+9	Command+9
Open or close Effect Controls panel for selected layer	F3 or Ctrl+Shift+T	F3 or Command+Shift+T
Open Flowchart panel for project flowchart	Ctrl+F11	Command+F11
Switch to workspace	Shift+F10, Shift+F11, or Shift+F12	Shift+F10, Shift+F11, or Shift+F12
Close active viewer or panel (closes content first)	Ctrl+W	Command+W
Close active panel or all viewers of type of active viewer (closes content first). For example, if a	Ctrl+Shift+W	Command+Shift+W

Timeline panel is active, this command closes all Timeline panels.		
Split the frame containing the active viewer and create a new viewer with opposite locked/unlo cked state	Ctrl+Alt+Shif t+N	Command+Option+S hift+N
Maximize or restore panel under pointer	` (accent grave)	` (accent grave)
Resize application window or floating window to fit screen. (Press again to resize window so that contents	Ctrl+\ (backslash)	Command+\ (backslash)

fill the screen.)		
Move application window or floating window to main monitor; resize window to fit screen. (Press again to resize window so that contents fill the screen.)	Ctrl+Alt+\ (backslash)	Command+Option+\ (backslash)
Toggle activation between Composition panel and Timeline panel for current composition	\ (backslash)	\ (backslash)
Cycle to previous or next item in active viewer	Shift+, (comma) or Shift+. (period)	Shift+, (comma) or Shift+. (period)

(for example, cycle through open composition s)		
Cycle to previous or next panel in active frame (for example, cycle through open Timeline panels)	Alt+Shift+, (comma) or Alt+Shift+. (period)	Option+Shift+, (comma) or Option+Shift+. (period)
Activate a view in a multi-view layout in the Composition panel without affecting layer selection	Click with middle mouse button	Click with middle mouse button

Activate Tools.

Note:

You can activate some tools only under certain circumstances. For example, you can activate a camera tool only when the active composition contains a camera layer.

Note:

To momentarily activate a tool with a single-letter keyboard shortcut, hold down the key; release the key to return to the previously active tool. To activate a tool and keep it active, press the key and immediately release it.

Result	Windows Shortcut	Mac OS Shortcut
Cycle through tools	Alt-click tool button in Tools panel	Option-click tool button in Tools panel
Activate Selection tool	V	V
Activate Hand tool	H	H
Temporarily activate Hand tool	Hold down spacebar or the middle mouse button	Hold down spacebar or the middle mouse button

Activate Zoom In tool	Z	Z
Activate Zoom Out tool	Alt (when Zoom In tool is active)	Option (when Zoom In tool is active)
Activate Rotation tool	W	W
Activate Roto Brush tool	Alt+W	Option+W
Activate Refine Edge tool	Alt+W	Option+W
Activate and cycle through Camera tools (Unified Camera, Orbit Camera, Track XY Camera, and Track Z Camera)	C	C
Activate Pan Behind tool	Y	Y
Activate and cycle through mask and shape tools (Rectangle, Rounded Rectangle, Ellipse, Polygon, Star)	Q	Q

Activate and cycle through Type tools (Horizontal and Vertical)	Ctrl+T	Command+T
Activate and cycle between the Pen and Mask Feather tools. (Note: You can turn off this setting in the Preferences dialog box.)	G	G
Temporarily activate Selection tool when a pen tool is selected	Ctrl	Command
Temporarily activate Pen tool when the Selection tool is selected and pointer is over a path (Add Vertex tool when pointer is over a segment; Convert Vertex tool when	Ctrl+Alt	Command+Option

pointer is over a vertex)		
Activate and cycle through Brush, Clone Stamp, and Eraser tools	Ctrl+B	Command+B
Activate and cycle through Puppet tools	Ctrl+P	Command+P
Temporarily convert Selection tool to Shape Duplication tool	Alt (in shape layer)	Option (in shape layer)
Temporarily convert Selection tool to Direct Selection tool	Ctrl (in shape layer)	Command (in shape layer)

Compositions and the Work Area.

Result	Windows Shortcut	Mac OS Shortcut
New composition	Ctrl+N	Command+N
Open Composition Settings dialog box for	Ctrl+K	Command+K

selected composition		
Set beginning or end of work area to current time	B or N	B or N
Set work area to duration of selected layers or, if no layers are selected, set work area to composition duration	Ctrl+Alt+B	Command+Option+B
Open Composition Mini-Flowchart for active composition	Tab	Tab
Activate the most recently active composition that is in the same composition hierarchy (network of nested	Shift+Esc	Shift+Esc

compositions) as the currently active composition		
Trim Composition to work area	Ctrl+Shift+X	Command+Shift+X
New Composition from selection	Alt+\	Option+\

Time Navigation.

Result	Windows Shortcut	Mac OS Shortcut
Go to specific time	Alt+Shift+J	Option+Shift+J
Go to beginning or end of work area	Shift+Home or Shift+End	Shift+Home or Shift+End
Go to previous or next visible item in time	J or K	J or K

ruler (keyframe, layer marker, work area beginning or end) (Note: Also goes to beginning, end, or base frame of Roto Brush span if viewing Roto Brush in Layer panel.)		
Go to beginning of composition, layer, or	Home or Ctrl+Alt+Left Arrow	Home or Command+Option+Left Arrow

footage item		
Go to end of composit ion, layer, or footage item	End or Ctrl+Alt+Right Arrow	End or Command+Option+Ri ght Arrow
Go forward 1 frame	Page Down or Ctrl+Right Arrow	Page Down or Command+Right Arrow
Go forward 10 frames	Shift+Page Down or Ctrl+Shift+Rig ht Arrow	Shift+Page Down or Command+Shift+Righ t Arrow
Go backwar d 1 frame	Page Up or Ctrl+Left Arrow	Page Up or Command+Left Arrow
Go backwar d 10 frames	Shift+Page Up or Ctrl+Shift+Left Arrow	Shift+Page Up or Command+Shift+Left Arrow
Go to layer In point	I	I
Go to layer Out point	O	O
Go to previous	Ctrl+Alt+Shift +Left Arrow	Command+Option+Sh ift+Left Arrow

In point or Out point		
Go to next In point or Out point	Ctrl+Alt+Shift +Right Arrow	Command+Option+Sh ift+Right Arrow
Scroll to current time in Timeline panel	D	D

Previews.

Result	Windows Shortcut	Mac OS Shortcut
Start or stop preview	Spacebar, o on numeric keypad, Shift+o on numeric keypad	Spacebar, o on numeric keypad, Shift+o on numeric keypad
Reset preview settings to replicate RAM Preview and Standard	Alt-click Reset in Preview panel	Option-click Reset in Preview panel

Preview behaviors		
Preview only audio, from current time	. (decimal point) on numeric keypad*	. (decimal point) on numeric keypad* or Control+. (period) on main keyboard
Preview only audio, in work area	Alt+. (decimal point) on numeric keypad*	Option+. (decimal point) on numeric keypad* or Control+Option+. (period) on main keyboard
Manually preview (scrub) video	Drag or Alt-drag current-time indicator, depending on Live Update setting	Drag or Option-drag current-time indicator, depending on Live Update setting
Manually preview (scrub) audio	Ctrl-drag current-time indicator	Command-drag current-time indicator
Preview number of frames specified by Alternate Preview preference	Alt+o on numeric keypad*	Option+o on numeric keypad* or Control+Option+o (zero) on main keyboard

(defaults to 5)		
Toggle Mercury Transmit video preview	/ (on numeric keypad)	/ (on numeric keypad), Control+/ on main keyboard
Take snapshot	Shift+F5, Shift+F6, Shift+F7, or Shift+F8	Shift+F5, Shift+F6, Shift+F7, or Shift+F8
Display snapshot in active viewer	F5, F6, F7, or F8	F5, F6, F7, or F8
Purge snapshot	Ctrl+Shift+F5, Ctrl+Shift+F6, Ctrl+Shift+F7, or Ctrl+Shift+F8	Command+Shift+F5, Command+Shift+F6, Command+Shift+F7, or Command+Shift+F8
Fast Previews > Off	Ctrl+Alt+1	Command+Option+1
Fast Previews > Adaptive Resolution	Ctrl+Alt+2	Command+Option+2
Fast Previews > Draft	Ctrl+Alt+3	Command+Option+3

Fast Previews > Fast Draft	Ctrl+Alt+4	Command+Option+4
Fast Previews > Wireframe	Ctrl+Alt+5	Command+Option+5

Note:

Some shortcuts are marked with an asterisk (*) to remind you to make sure that Num Lock is on when you use the numeric keypad.

Views

Result	Windows Shortcut	Mac OS Shortcut
Turn display color management on or off for active view	Shift+/ (on numeric keypad)	Shift+/ (on numeric keypad)
Show red, green, blue, or alpha channel as grayscale	Alt+1, Alt+2, Alt+3, Alt+4	Option+1, Option+2, Option+3, Option+4

Show colorized red, green, or blue channel	Alt+Shift+1, Alt+Shift+2, Alt+Shift+3	Option+Shift+1, Option+Shift+2, Option+Shift+3
Toggle showing straight RGB color	Alt+Shift+4	Option+Shift+4
Show alpha boundary (outline between transparent and opaque regions) in Layer panel	Alt+5	Option+5
Show alpha overlay (colored overlay on transparent regions) in Layer panel	Alt+6	Option+6
Show Refine Edge X-ray	Alt+X	Option+X
Center composition in the panel	Double-click Hand tool	Double-click Hand tool

Zoom-in in Composition, Layer, or Footage panel	. (period) on main keyboard	. (period) on main keyboard
Zoom-out in Composition, Layer, or Footage panel	, (comma)	, (comma)
Zoom to 100% in Composition, Layer, or Footage panel	/ (on main keyboard)	/ (on main keyboard)
Zoom to fit in Composition, Layer, or Footage panel	Shift+/ (on main keyboard)	Shift+/ (on main keyboard)
Zoom up to 100% to fit in Composition, Layer, or Footage panel	Alt+/ (on main keyboard)	Option+/ (on main keyboard)

Set resolution to Full, Half, or Custom in Composition panel	Ctrl+J, Ctrl+Shift+J, Ctrl+Alt+J	Command+J, Command+Shift+J, Command+Option+J
Open View Options dialog box for active Composition panel	Ctrl+Alt+U	Command+Option+U
Zoom in time	= (equal sign) on main keyboard	= (equal sign) on main keyboard
Zoom out time	- (hyphen) on main keyboard	- (hyphen) on main keyboard
Zoom in Timeline panel to single-frame units (Press again to zoom out to show entire composition duration.)	; (semicolon)	; (semicolon)

Zoom out in Timeline panel to show the entire composition duration (Press again to zoom back in to the duration specified by the Time Navigator.)	Shift+; (semicolon)	Shift+; (semicolon)
Prevent images from being rendered for previews in viewer panels	Caps Lock	Caps Lock
Show or hide safe zones	' (apostrophe)	' (apostrophe)
Show or hide grid	Ctrl+' (apostrophe)	Command+' (apostrophe)
Show or hide	Alt+' (apostrophe)	Option+' (apostrophe)

proportional grid		
Show or hide rulers	Ctrl+R	Command+R
Show or hide guides	Ctrl+; (semicolon)	Command+; (semicolon)
Turn snapping to grid on or off	Ctrl+Shift+' (apostrophe)	Command+Shift+' (apostrophe)
Turn snapping to guides on or off	Ctrl+Shift+; (semicolon)	Command+Shift+; (semicolon)
Lock or unlock guides	Ctrl+Alt+Shift +; (semicolon)	Command+Option+Shift+; (semicolon)
Show or hide layer controls (masks, motion paths, light and camera wireframes, effect control points, and layer handles)	Ctrl+Shift+H	Command+Shift+H

Footage.

Result	Windows Shortcut	Mac OS Shortcut
Import one file or image sequence	Ctrl+I	Command+I
Import multiple files or image sequences	Ctrl+Alt+I	Command+Option+I
Open movie in an After Effects Footage panel	Double-click the footage item in the Project panel	Double-click the footage item in the Project panel
Add selected items to most recently activated composition	Ctrl+/ (on main keyboard)	Command+/ (on main keyboard)
Replace selected source footage for selected layers with footage item selected in Project panel	Ctrl+Alt+/ (on main keyboard)	Command+Option+/ (on main keyboard)

Replace source for a selected layer	Alt-drag footage item from Project panel onto selected layer	Option-drag footage item from Project panel onto selected layer
Delete a footage item without a warning	Ctrl+Backspace e	Command+Delete
Open Interpret Footage dialog box for selected footage item	Ctrl+Alt+G	Command+Option+G
Remember footage interpretatio n	Ctrl+Alt+C	Command+Option+C
Edit selected footage item in application with which it's associated (Edit Original)	Ctrl+E	Command+E
Replace selected footage item	Ctrl+H	Command+H

Reload selected footage items	Ctrl+Alt+L	Command+Option+L
Set proxy for selected footage item	Ctrl+Alt+P	Command+Option+P

Effects and Animation Presets.

Result	Windows Shortcut	Mac OS Shortcut
Delete all effects from selected layers	Ctrl+Shift+E	Command+Shift+E
Apply most recently applied effect to selected layers	Ctrl+Alt+Shift+E	Command+Option+Shift+E
Apply most recently applied animatio	Ctrl+Alt+Shift+F	Command+Option+Shift+F

n preset to selected layers		

Layers.

Note:

Some operations do not affect shy layers.

Result	Windows Shortcut	Mac OS Shortcut
New solid layer	Ctrl+Y	Command+Y
New null layer	Ctrl+Alt+Shift+Y	Command+Option+Shift+Y
New adjustment layer	Ctrl+Alt+Y	Command+Option+Y
Select layer (1-999) by its number (enter digits rapidly for two-digit and three-digit numbers)	0-9 on numeric keypad*	0-9 on numeric keypad*

Toggle selection of layer (1-999) by its number (enter digits rapidly for two-digit and three-digit numbers)	Shift+0-9 on numeric keypad*	Shift+0-9 on numeric keypad*
Select next layer in stacking order	Ctrl+Down Arrow	Command+Down Arrow
Select previous layer in stacking order	Ctrl+Up Arrow	Command+Up Arrow
Extend selection to next layer in stacking order	Ctrl+Shift+Down Arrow	Command+Shift+Down Arrow
Extend selection to previous layer in stacking order	Ctrl+Shift+Up Arrow	Command+Shift+Up Arrow

Deselect all layers	Ctrl+Shift+A	Command+Shift+A
Scroll topmost selected layer to top of Timeline panel	X	X
Show or hide Parent column	Shift+F4	Shift+F4
Show or hide Layer Switches and Modes columns	F4	F4
Setting the sampling method for selected layers (Best/Bilinear)	Alt+B	Option+B
Setting the sampling method for selected layers (Best/Bicubic)	Alt+Shift+B	Option+Shift+B

Turn off all other solo switches	Alt-click solo switch	Option-click solo switch
Turn Video (eyeball) switch on or off for selected layers	Ctrl+Alt+Shift+V	Command+Option+Shift+V
Turn off Video switch for all video layers other than selected layers	Ctrl+Shift+V	Command+Shift+V
Open settings dialog box for selected solid, light, camera, null, or adjustment layer	Ctrl+Shift+Y	Command+Shift+Y
Paste layers at current time	Ctrl+Alt+V	Command+Option+V
Split selected	Ctrl+Shift+D	Command+Shift+D

layers. (If no layers are selected, split all layers.)		
Precompose selected layers	Ctrl+Shift+C	Command+Shift+C
Open Effect Controls panel for selected layers	Ctrl+Shift+T	Command+Shift+T
Open layer in Layer panel (opens source composition for precomposi tion layer in Compositio n panel)	Double-click a layer	Double-click a layer
Open source of a layer in Footage panel (opens precomposi	Alt-double-click a layer	Option-double-click a layer

tion layer in Layer panel)		
Reverse selected layers in time	Ctrl+Alt+R	Command+Option+R
Enable time remapping for selected layers	Ctrl+Alt+T	Command+Option+T
Move selected layers so that their In point or Out point is at the current time	[(left bracket) or] (right bracket)	[(left bracket) or] (right bracket)
Trim In point or Out point of selected layers to current time	Alt+[(left bracket) or Alt+] (right bracket)	Option+[(left bracket) or Option+] (right bracket)
Add or remove expression for a property	Alt-click stopwatch	Option-click stopwatch

Add an effect (or multiple selected effects) to selected layers	Double-click effect selection in Effects & Presets panel	Double-click effect selection in Effects & Presets panel
Set In point or Out point by time-stretching	Ctrl+Shift+, (comma) or Ctrl+Alt+, (comma)	Command+Shift+, (comma) or Command+Option+, (comma)
Move selected layers so that their In point is at beginning of composition	Alt+Home	Option+Home
Move selected layers so that their Out point is at end of composition	Alt+End	Option+End
Lock selected layers	Ctrl+L	Command+L
Unlock all layers	Ctrl+Shift+L	Command+Shift+L

Set Quality to Best, Draft, or Wireframe for selected layers	Ctrl+U, Ctrl+Shift+U, or Ctrl+Alt+Shift+U	Command+U, Command+Shift+U, Command+Option+Shift+U
Cycle forward or backward through blending modes for selected layers	Shift+- (hyphen) or Shift+= (equal sign) on the main keyboard	Shift+- (hyphen) or Shift+= (equal sign) on the main keyboard
Find in Timeline panel	Ctrl+F	Command+F

Note:

Some shortcuts are marked with an asterisk (*) to remind you to make sure that Num Lock is on when you use the numeric keypad.

Showing Properties and Groups in the Timeline Panel.

Note:

This table contains double-letter shortcuts (for example, LL). To use these shortcuts, press the letters in quick succession.

Result	Windows Shortcut	Mac OS Shortcut
Find in Timeline panel	Ctrl+F	Command+F
Toggle expansion of selected layers to show all properties	Ctrl+` (accent grave)	Command+` (accent grave)
Toggle expansion of property group and all child property groups to show all properties	Ctrl-click triangle to the left of the property group name	Command-click triangle to the left of the property group name
Show only Anchor Point property (for lights and cameras,	A	A

Point Of Interest)		
Show only Audio Levels property	L	L
Show only Mask Feather property	F	F
Show only Mask Path property	M	M
Show only Mask Opacity property	TT	TT
Show only Opacity property (for lights, Intensity)	T	T
Show only Position property	P	P
Show only Rotation and Orientation properties	R	R

Show only Scale property	S	S
Show only Time Remap property	RR	RR
Show only instances of missing effects	FF	FF
Show only Effects property group	E	E
Show only mask property groups	MM	MM
Show only Material Options property group	AA	AA
Show only expressions	EE	EE
Show properties with keyframes	U	U

Show only modified properties	UU	UU
Show only paint strokes, Roto Brush strokes, and Puppet pins	PP	PP
Show only audio waveform	LL	LL
Show only selected properties and groups	SS	SS
Hide property or group	Alt+Shift-click property or group name	Option+Shift-click property or group name
Add or remove property or group from set that is shown	Shift+property or group shortcut	Shift+property or group shortcut
Add or remove keyframe at current time	Alt+Shift+property shortcut	Option+property shortcut

Showing Properties in the Effect Controls Panel.

Result	Windows Shortcut	Mac OS Shortcut
Toggle expansion of selected effects to show all properties	Ctrl+` (accent grave)	Command+` (accent grave)
Toggle expansion of property group and all child property groups to show all properties	Ctrl-click triangle to the left of the property group name	Command-click triangle to the left of the property group name

Modifying Layer Properties.

Result	Windows Shortcut	Mac OS Shortcut
Modify property value by default increments	Drag property value	Drag property value
Modify property value by	Shift-drag property value	Shift-drag property value

10x default increments		
Modify property value by 1/10 default increments	Ctrl-drag property value	Command-drag property value
Open Auto-Orientation dialog box for selected layers	Ctrl+Alt+O	Command+Alt+O
Open Opacity dialog box for selected layers	Ctrl+Shift+O	Command+Shift+O
Open Rotation dialog box for selected layers	Ctrl+Shift+R	Command+Shift+R
Open Position dialog box for	Ctrl+Shift+P	Command+Shift+P

selected layers		
Center selected layers in view (modifies Position property to place anchor points of selected layers in center of current view)	Ctrl+Home	Command+Home
Center anchor point in the visible content	Ctrl+Alt+Ho me	Command+Option+H ome
Move selected layers 1 pixel at current magnificat ion (Position)	Arrow key	Arrow key

Move selected layers 10 pixels at current magnificat ion (Position)	Shift+arrow key	Shift+arrow key
Move selected layers 1 frame earlier or later	Alt+Page Up or Alt+Page Down	Option+Page Up or Option+Page Down
Move selected layers 10 frames earlier or later	Alt+Shift+Pag e Up or Alt+Shift+Pag e Down	Option+Shift+Page Up or Option+Shift+Page Down
Increase or decrease Rotation (Z Rotation) of selected layers by 1°	+ (plus) or - (minus) on numeric keypad	+ (plus) or - (minus) on numeric keypad
Increase or decrease Rotation (Z	Shift++ (plus) or Shift+- (minus) on	Shift++ (plus) or Shift+- (minus) on numeric keypad

Rotation) of selected layers by 10°	numeric keypad	
Increase or decrease Opacity (or Intensity for light layers) of selected layers by 1%	Ctrl+Alt++ (plus) or Ctrl+Alt+- (minus) on numeric keypad	Control+Option++ (plus) or Control+Option+- (minus) on numeric keypad
Increase or decrease Opacity (or Intensity for light layers) of selected layers by 10%	Ctrl+Alt+Shift++ (plus) or Ctrl+Alt+Shift+- (minus) on numeric keypad	Control+Option+Shift++ (plus) or Control+Option+Shift+- (minus) on numeric keypad
Increase Scale of selected layers by 1%	Ctrl++ (plus) or Alt++ (plus) on numeric keypad	Command++ (plus) or Option++ (plus) on numeric keypad
Decrease Scale of selected	Ctrl+- (minus) or Alt+- (minus)	Command+- (minus) or Option+- (minus) on numeric keypad

layers by 1%	on numeric keypad	
Increase Scale of selected layers by 10%	Ctrl+Shift++ (plus) or Alt+Shift++ (plus) on numeric keypad	Command+Shift++ (plus) or Option+Shift++ (plus) on numeric keypad
Decrease Scale of selected layers by 10%	Ctrl+Shift+- (minus) or Alt+Shift+- (minus) on numeric keypad	Command+Shift+- (minus) or Option+Shift+- (minus) on numeric keypad
Modify Rotation or Orientatio n in 45° increments	Shift-drag with Rotation tool	Shift-drag with Rotation tool
Modify Scale, constraine d to footage frame aspect ratio	Shift-drag layer handle with Selection tool	Shift-drag layer handle with Selection tool
Reset Rotation to 0°	Double-click Rotation tool	Double-click Rotation tool

Reset Scale to 100%	Double-click Selection tool	Double-click Selection tool
Scale and reposition selected layers to fit composition	Ctrl+Alt+F	Command+Option+F
Scale and reposition selected layers to fit composition width, preserving image aspect ratio for each layer	Ctrl+Alt+Shift+H	Command+Option+Shift+H
Scale and reposition selected layers to fit composition height, preserving image aspect ratio for each layer	Ctrl+Alt+Shift+G	Command+Option+Shift+G

3D Layers.

Note:

(Mac OS) Shortcuts involving function keys F9-F12 may conflict with shortcuts used by the operating system. See Mac OS Help for instructions to reassign Dashboard & Expose shortcuts.

Result	Windows Shortcut	Mac OS Shortcut
Switch to 3D view 1 (defaults to Front)	F10	F10
Switch to 3D view 2 (defaults to Custom View 1)	F11	F11
Switch to 3D view 3 (defaults to Active	F12	F12

Camera)		
Return to previou s view	Esc	Esc
New light	Ctrl+Alt+Shift +L	Command+Option+Shift +L
New camera	Ctrl+Alt+Shift +C	Command+Option+Shift +C
Move the camera and its point of interest to look at selecte d 3D layers	Ctrl+Alt+Shift +\	Command+Option+Shift +\
With a camera tool selecte d, move the camera and its point of interest	F	F

to look at selecte d 3D layers		
With a camera tool selecte d, move the camera and its point of interest to look at all 3D layers	Ctrl+Shift+F	Command+Shift+F
Turn Casts Shadow s propert y on or off for selecte d 3D layers	Alt+Shift+C	Option+Shift+C

Keyframes and the Graph Editor

Note:

(Mac OS) Shortcuts involving function keys F9-F12 may conflict with shortcuts used by the operating system. See Mac OS Help for instructions to reassign Dashboard & Expose shortcuts.

Result	Windows Shortcut	Mac OS Shortcut
Toggle between Graph Editor and layer bar modes	Shift+F3	Shift+F3
Select all keyframes for a property	Click property name	Click property name
Select all visible keyframes and properties	Ctrl+Alt+A	Command+Option+A
Deselect all keyframes, properties	Shift+F2 or Ctrl+Alt+Shift+A	Shift+F2 or Command+Option+Shift+A

, and property groups		
Move keyframe 1 frame later or earlier	Alt+Right Arrow or Alt+Left Arrow	Option+Right Arrow or Option+Left Arrow
Move keyframe 10 frames later or earlier	Alt+Shift+Right Arrow or Alt+Shift+Left Arrow	Option+Shift+Right Arrow or Option+Shift+Left Arrow
Set interpolation for selected keyframes (layer bar mode)	Ctrl+Alt+K	Command+Option+K
Set keyframe interpolation method to hold or Auto Bezier	Ctrl+Alt+H	Command+Option+H
Set keyframe interpolati	Ctrl-click in layer bar mode	Command-click in layer bar mode

on method to linear or Auto Bezier		
Set keyframe interpolation method to linear or hold	Ctrl+Alt-click in layer bar mode	Command+Option-click in layer bar mode
Easy ease selected keyframes	F9	F9
Easy ease selected keyframes in	Shift+F9	Shift+F9
Easy ease selected keyframes out	Ctrl+Shift+F9	Command+Shift+F9
Set velocity for selected keyframes	Ctrl+Shift+K	Command+Shift+K
Add or remove keyframe	Alt+Shift+property shortcut	Option+property shortcut

at current time. For property shortcuts		

Text.

Result	Windows Shortcut	Mac OS Shortcut
New text layer	Ctrl+Alt+Shift+T	Command+Option+Shift+T
Align selected horizontal text left, center, or right	Ctrl+Shift+L, Ctrl+Shift+C, or Ctrl+Shift+R	Command+Shift+L, Command+Shift+C, or Command+Shift+R
Align selected vertical text top, center, or bottom	Ctrl+Shift+L, Ctrl+Shift+C, or Ctrl+Shift+R	Command+Shift+L, Command+Shift+C, or Command+Shift+R
Extend or reduce selectio	Shift+Right Arrow or Shift+Left Arrow	Shift+Right Arrow or Shift+Left Arrow

n by one characte r to right or left in horizont al text		
Extend or reduce selectio n by one word to right or left in horizont al text	Ctrl+Shift+Rig ht Arrow or Ctrl+Shift+Left Arrow	Command+Shift+Right Arrow or Command+Shift+Left Arrow
Extend or reduce selectio n by one line up or down in horizont al text	Shift+Up Arrow or Shift+Down Arrow	Shift+Up Arrow or Shift+Down Arrow
Extend or reduce selectio	Shift+Right Arrow or Shift+Left Arrow	Shift+Right Arrow or Shift+Left Arrow

n by one line to right or left in vertical text		
Extend or reduce selectio n one word up or down in vertical text	Ctrl+Shift+Up Arrow or Ctrl+Shift+Dow n Arrow	Command+Shift+Up Arrow or Command+Shift+Down Arrow
Extend or reduce selectio n by one characte r up or down in vertical text	Shift+Up Arrow or Shift+Down Arrow	Shift+Up Arrow or Shift+Down Arrow
Select text from insertio n point	Shift+Home or Shift+End	Shift+Home or Shift+End

to beginni ng or end of line		
Move insertio n point to beginni ng or end of line	Home or End	Home or End
Select all text on a layer	Double-click text layer	Double-click text layer
Select text from insertio n point to beginni ng or end of text frame	Ctrl+Shift+Ho me or Ctrl+Shift+End	Command+Shift+Hom e or Command+Shift+End
Select text from	Shift-click	Shift-click

insertion point to mouse-click point		
In horizontal text, move insertion point one character left or right; one line up or down; one word left or right; or one paragraph up or down	Left Arrow or Right Arrow; Up Arrow or Down Arrow; Ctrl+Left Arrow or Ctrl+Right Arrow; or Ctrl+Up Arrow or Ctrl+Down Arrow	Left Arrow or Right Arrow; Up Arrow or Down Arrow; Command+Left Arrow or Command+Right Arrow; or Command+Up Arrow or Command+Down Arrow
In vertical text, move	Up Arrow or Down Arrow; Left Arrow or Right Arrow;	Up Arrow or Down Arrow; Left Arrow or Right Arrow; Command+Up Arrow

insertio n point one characte r up or down; one left or right; one word up or down; or one paragra ph left or right	Ctrl+Up Arrow or Ctrl+Down Arrow; or Ctrl+Left Arrow or Ctrl+Right Arrow	or Command+Down Arrow; or Command+Left Arrow or Command+Right Arrow
Select word, line, paragra ph, or entire text frame	Double-click, triple-click, quadruple-click, or quintuple-click with Type tool	Double-click, triple-click, quadruple-click, or quintuple-click with Type tool
Turn All Caps on or off for selected text	Ctrl+Shift+K	Command+Shift+K
Turn Small	Ctrl+Alt+Shift+ K	Command+Option+Shi ft+K

Caps on or off for selected text		
Turn Supersc ript on or off for selected text	Ctrl+Shift+= (equal sign)	Command+Shift+= (equal sign)
Turn Subscri pt on or off for selected text	Ctrl+Alt+Shift+ = (equal sign)	Command+Option+Shi ft+= (equal sign)
Set horizont al scale to 100% for selected text	Ctrl+Shift+X	Command+Shift+X
Set vertical scale to 100% for selected text	Ctrl+Alt+Shift+ X	Command+Option+Shi ft+X

Auto leading for selected text	Ctrl+Alt+Shift+A	Command+Option+Shift+A
Reset tracking to 0 for selected text	Ctrl+Shift+Q	Command+Shift+Control+Q
Justify paragraph; left align last line	Ctrl+Shift+J	Command+Shift+J
Justify paragraph; right align last line	Ctrl+Alt+Shift+J	Command+Option+Shift+J
Justify paragraph; force last line	Ctrl+Shift+F	Command+Shift+F
Decrease or increase font size of	Ctrl+Shift+, (comma) or Ctrl+Shift+. (period)	Command+Shift+, (comma) or Command+Shift+. (period)

selected text by 2 units		
Decrease or increase font size of selected text by 10 units	Ctrl+Alt+Shift+, (comma) or Ctrl+Alt+Shift+. (period)	Command+Option+Shift+, (comma) or Command+Option+Shift+. (period)
Increase or decrease leading by 2 units	Alt+Down Arrow or Alt+Up Arrow	Option+Down Arrow or Option+Up Arrow
Increase or decrease leading by 10 units	Ctrl+Alt+Down Arrow or Ctrl+Alt+Up Arrow	Command+Option+Down Arrow or Command+Option+Up Arrow
Decrease or increase baseline shift by 2 units	Alt+Shift+Down Arrow or Alt+Shift+Up Arrow	Option+Shift+Down Arrow or Option+Shift+Up Arrow

Decrease or increase baseline shift by 10 units	Ctrl+Alt+Shift+ Down Arrow or Ctrl+Alt+Shift+ Up Arrow	Command+Option+Shi ft+Down Arrow or Command+Option+Shi ft+Up Arrow
Decrease or increase kerning or tracking 20 units (20/100 0 ems)	Alt+Left Arrow or Alt+Right Arrow	Option+Left Arrow or Option+Right Arrow
Decrease or increase kerning or tracking 100 units (100/10 00 ems)	Ctrl+Alt+Left Arrow or Ctrl+Alt+Right Arrow	Command+Option+Lef t Arrow or Command+Option+Rig ht Arrow
Toggle paragra ph compos er	Ctrl+Alt+Shift+ T	Command+Option+Shi ft+T

Masks.

Result	Windows Shortcut	Mac OS Shortcut
New mask	Ctrl+Shift+N	Command+Shift+N
Select all points in a mask	Alt-click mask	Option-click mask
Select next or previous mask	Alt+` (accent grave) or Alt+Shift+` (accent grave)	Option+` (accent grave) or Option+Shift+` (accent grave)
Enter free-transform mask editing mode	Double-click mask with Selection tool or select mask in Timeline panel and press Ctrl+T	Double-click mask with Selection tool or select mask in Timeline panel and press Command+T
Exit free-transform mask editing mode	Esc	Esc
Scale around center point in Free Transform mode	Ctrl-drag	Command-drag
Move selected path points 1 pixel at	Arrow key	Arrow key

current magnification		
Move selected path points 10 pixels at current magnification	Shift+arrow key	Shift+arrow key
Toggle between smooth and corner points	Ctrl+Alt-click vertex	Command+Option-click vertex
Redraw Bezier handles	Ctrl+Alt-drag vertex	Command+Option-drag vertex
Invert selected mask	Ctrl+Shift+I	Command+Shift+I
Open Mask Feather dialog box for selected mask	Ctrl+Shift+F	Command+Shift+F
Open Mask Shape dialog box for selected mask	Ctrl+Shift+M	Command+Shift+M

Paint Tools.

Result	Windows Shortcut	Mac OS Shortcut

Swap paint background color and foreground colors	X	X
Set paint foreground color to black and background color to white	D	D
Set foreground color to the color currently under any paint tool pointer	Alt-click	Option-click
Set foreground color to the average color of a 4-pixel x 4-pixel area under any paint tool pointer	Ctrl+Alt-click	Command+Option-click
Set brush size for a paint tool	Ctrl-drag	Command-drag
Set brush hardness for a paint tool	Ctrl-drag, then release Ctrl while dragging	Command-drag, then release Command while dragging
Join current paint stroke to	Hold Shift while	Hold Shift while beginning stroke

the previous stroke	beginning stroke	
Set starting sample point to point currently under Clone Stamp tool pointer	Alt-click	Option-click
Momentarily activate Eraser tool with Last Stroke Only option	Ctrl+Shift	Command+Shift
Show and move overlay (change Offset value of *aligned* Clone Stamp tool or change Source Position value of *unaligned* Clone Stamp tool)	Alt+Shift-drag with Clone Stamp tool	Option+Shift-drag with Clone Stamp tool
Activate a specific Clone Stamp tool preset	3, 4, 5, 6, or 7 on the main keyboard	3, 4, 5, 6, or 7 on the main keyboard
Duplicate a Clone Stamp tool preset in Paint panel	Alt-click the button for the preset	Option-click the button for the preset

Set opacity for a paint tool	Digit on numeric keypad (for example, 9=90%, 1=10%)*	Digit on numeric keypad (for example, 9=90%, 1=10%)*
Set opacity for a paint tool to 100%	. (decimal) on numeric keypad*	. (decimal) on numeric keypad*
Set flow for a paint tool	Shift+ a digit on numeric keypad (for example, 9=90%, 1=10%)*	Shift+ a digit on numeric keypad (for example, 9=90%, 1=10%)*
Set flow for a paint tool to 100%	Shift+. (decimal) on numeric keypad*	Shift+. (decimal) on numeric keypad*
Move earlier or later by number of frames specified for stroke Duration	Ctrl+Page Up or Ctrl+Page Down (or 1 or 2 on the main keyboard)	Command+Page Up or Command+Page Down (or 1 or 2 on the main keyboard)

Note:

Some shortcuts are marked with an asterisk (*) to remind you to make sure that Num Lock is on when you use the numeric keypad.

Shape Layers.

Result	Windows Shortcut	Mac OS Shortcut
Group selected shapes	Ctrl+G	Command+G
Ungroup selected shapes	Ctrl+Shift+G	Command+Shift+G
Enter free-transform path editing mode	Select Path property in Timeline panel and press Ctrl+T	Select Path property in Timeline panel and press Command+T
Increase star inner roundness	Page Up when dragging to create shape	Page Up when dragging to create shape
Decrease star inner roundness	Page Down when dragging to create shape	Page Down when dragging to create shape
Increase number of points for star or	Up Arrow when dragging to create shape	Up Arrow when dragging to create shape

polygon; increase roundness for rounded rectangle		
Decrease number of points for star or polygon; decrease roundness for rounded rectangle	Down Arrow when dragging to create shape	Down Arrow when dragging to create shape
Reposition shape during creation	Hold spacebar when dragging to create shape	Hold spacebar when dragging to create shape
Set rounded rectangle roundness to 0 (sharp corners); decrease polygon and star outer roundness	Left Arrow when dragging to create shape	Left Arrow when dragging to create shape
Set rounded rectangle roundness to maximum;	Right Arrow when dragging to create shape	Right Arrow when dragging to create shape

increase polygon and star outer roundness		
Constrain rectangles to squares; constrain ellipses to circles; constrain polygons and stars to zero rotation	Shift when dragging to create shape	Shift when dragging to create shape
Change outer radius of star	Ctrl when dragging to create shape	Command when dragging to create shape

Markers.

Result	Windows Shortcut	Mac OS Shortcut
Set marker at current time (works during preview and audio-only preview)	* (multiply) on numeric keypad	* (multiply) on numeric keypad or Control+8 on main keyboard
Set marker at current time	Alt+* (multiply)	Option+* (multiply) on numeric keypad or

and open marker dialog box	on numeric keypad	Control+Option+8 on main keyboard
Set and number a composition marker (0-9) at the current time	Shift+0-9 on main keyboard	Shift+0-9 on main keyboard
Go to a composition marker (0-9)	0-9 on main keyboard	0-9 on main keyboard
Display the duration between two layer markers or keyframes in the Info panel	Alt-click the markers or keyframes	Option-click the markers or keyframes
Remove marker	Ctrl-click marker	Command-click marker

Motion Tracking.

Result	Windows Shortcut	Mac OS Shortcut
Move feature region, search region, and attach point 1	Arrow key	Arrow key

pixel at current magnificatio n		
Move feature region, search region, and attach point 10 pixels at current magnificatio n	Shift+arrow key	Shift+arrow key
Move feature region and search region 1 pixel at current magnificatio n	Alt+arrow key	Option+arrow key
Move feature region and search region 10 pixels at current magnificatio n	Alt+Shift+arro w key	Option+Shift+arro w key

Saving, Exporting, and Rendering.

Result	Windows Shortcut	Mac OS Shortcut
Save project	Ctrl+S	Command+S
Increment and save project	Ctrl+Alt+Shift +S	Command+Option+Shi ft+S
Save As	Ctrl+Shift+S	Command+Shift+S
Add active compositi on or selected items to render queue	Ctrl+Shift+/ (on main keyboard)	Command+Shift+/ (on main keyboard)
Add current frame to render queue	Ctrl+Alt+S	Command+Option+S
Duplicate render item with same output filename as original	Ctrl+Shift+D	Command+Shift+D
Add a compositi	Ctrl+Alt+M	Cmd+Option+M

on to the Adobe Media Encoder encoding queue		

Note:

On Mac OS, some keyboard commands used to interact with the operating system conflict with keyboard commands for interacting with After Effects. Select Use System Shortcut Keys in the General preferences to override the After Effects keyboard command in some cases in which there's a conflict with the Mac OS keyboard command.

Applies to: Adobe After Effects.

Customer's Page.

This page is for customers who enjoyed Adobe After Effects Keyboard Shortcuts for Windows and Macintosh.

Our beloved and respectable reader, we thank you very much for your patronage. Please we will appreciate it more if you rate and review this book; that is if it was helpful to you. Thank you.

Download Our EBooks Today For Free.

In order to appreciate our customers, we have made some of our titles available at 0.00. They are totally free. Feel free to get a copy of the free titles.

Here are books we give to our customers free of charge:

(A) For Keyboard Shortcuts in Windows check:

Windows 7 Keyboard Shortcuts.

(B) For Keyboard Shortcuts in Office 2016 for Windows check:

<u>Word 2016</u> Keyboard Shortcuts For Windows.

(C) For Keyboard Shortcuts in Office 2016 for Mac check:

<u>OneNote 2016</u> Keyboard Shortcuts For Macintosh.

Follow <u>this link</u> to download any of the titles listed above for free.

Note: Feel free to download them from our website or your favorite bookstore today. Thank you.

Other Books By This Publisher.

Titles for single programs under Shortcut Matters Series are not part of this list.

S/N	Title	Series
Series A: Limits Breaking Quotes.		
1	Discover Your Key Christian Quotes	Limits Breaking Quotes
Series B: Shortcut Matters.		
1	Windows 7 Shortcuts	Shortcut Matters
2	Windows 7 Shortcuts & Tips	Shortcut Matters
3	Windows 8.1 Shortcuts	Shortcut Matters
4	Windows 10 Shortcut Keys	Shortcut Matters
5	Microsoft Office 2007 Keyboard Shortcuts For Windows.	Shortcut Matters
6	Microsoft Office 2010 Shortcuts For Windows.	Shortcut Matters
7	Microsoft Office 2013 Shortcuts For Windows.	Shortcut Matters
8	Microsoft Office 2016 Shortcuts For Windows.	Shortcut Matters
9	Microsoft Office 2016 Keyboard Shortcuts For Macintosh.	Shortcut Matters
10	Top 11 Adobe Programs Keyboard Shortcuts	Shortcut Matters
11	Top 10 Email Service Providers Keyboard Shortcuts	Shortcut Matters
12	Hot Corel Programs Keyboard Shortcuts	Shortcut Matters

13	Top 10 Browsers Keyboard Shortcuts	Shortcut Matters
14	Microsoft Browsers Keyboard Shortcuts.	Shortcut Matters
15	Popular Email Service Providers Keyboard Shortcuts	Shortcut Matters
16	Professional Video Editing with Keyboard Shortcuts.	Shortcut Matters
17	Popular Web Browsers Keyboard Shortcuts.	Shortcut Matters

Series C: Teach Yourself.

1	Teach Yourself Computer Fundamentals	Teach Yourself
2	Teach Yourself Computer Fundamentals Workbook	Teach Yourself

Series D: For Painless Publishing

1	Self-Publish it with CreateSpace.	For Painless Publishing
2	Where is my money? Now solved for Kindle and CreateSpace	For Painless Publishing
3	Describe it on Amazon	For Painless Publishing